Views of Old CORNWALL

Picture Postcards: Peter Dryden
Text: Sarah Foot

Mother Ivey's Bay, near Padstow.

Bossiney Books

First published in 1981
by Bossiney Books
St Teath, Bodmin, Cornwall
Designed, typeset and printed in Great Britain by
Penwell Ltd., Parkwood, Callington
Cornwall

Hardcover ISBN 0 906456 54 1
Paperback ISBN 0 906456 53 3

ABOUT THE AUTHORS

Peter Dryden, a Cornishman, was born at Penryn in 1946 and educated at Falmouth Grammar School. He has done a variety of jobs working in shops, cafes, a cinema, and for BBC TV as a projectionist in the dubbing theatre. He and his wife Angela and their two children, Georgina and Richard, now live in Brighton where he is the Officer in charge of a Home for the Elderly, having taken up Residential Social Work with the Elderly in 1975. 'I started collecting old picture postcards in 1969,' he recalls, 'when I could find anyone selling them. They used to cost 1d or 2d each . . . I even got given bundles by antique dealers who didn't know how to get rid of them! Moving to Brighton proved quite profitable as there were a lot of Postcard Fairs to attend and quite a few postcard dealers. I think I was the only person after Cornish cards for about three years . . . so I cornered the market. But now I rarely buy any as the prices have become prohibitive.'

Sarah Foot, who has written the text of this book, lives at St. Mellion, near Callington, with her husband and two children. Formerly on the staff of the 'London Evening News', she contributes regularly to 'The Western Morning News'. This is Sarah Foot's fourth title for Bossiney. In 1979 she wrote **Following the River Fowey,** a personal portrait of the lovely Fowey from its beginnings on Bodmin Moor down to the sea. Early in 1980 she completed **Following the Tamar,** an even longer journey in words and pictures. Both books were extremely well received.

Sarah Foot is the grand-daughter of that great Westcountry Liberal and Methodist Isaac Foot and in the autumn of 1980 her book **My Grandfather Isaac Foot** appeared, coinciding with a television documentary on the same subject. She is currently at work on **The Cornish Countryside,** a portrait of the Cornish landscape through the four seasons, scheduled to appear in 1982.

Sarah Foot

3

VIEWS OF OLD CORNWALL

Cross the River Tamar into Cornwall and you will immediately be aware of a great difference.

For Cornwall's heart is made from granite, tin and copper, and since mining and fishing were for years the mainstay of its people their characters have been, to a great extent, formed by these treacherous and arduous duties. Hard and flinty this county and its people may appear to the visitor, but once their individuality has captured your heart they will not let you go.

Nowhere that I know has the structure of the land so affected the people who live on it.

Cornwall has produced and enticed many artists and writers. There has recently been a revival of interest and appreciation of the Victorian artists who settled at Newlyn and St Ives and many great writers have been born or come to settle here. Notably Sir Arthur Quiller Couch who made his

◀ *East Pool Mine, Camborne*

home town of Fowey famous and Daphne du Maurier and Sir John Betjeman who write of Cornwall as only true lovers of this county can.

But Cornwall has also produced men of practical skills: engineers, boat-builders, stone masons and carpenters. She, too, has honoured and produced some fine orators. John Wesley came in the eighteenth century and gave hope and promise to the miners who worked for long and dreadful hours in the bowels of the earth. His followers built their little stone chapels across the county and here the great hymns were sung, the fine sermons preached; those 'tongues of angels' belonging to the Cornish people were loosed.

Legends were and still are greatly loved and meticulously handed down from one Cornish generation to another. King Arthur's spirit is alive and well in Tintagel. Tregeagle's ghost howls on Bodmin Moor. Giants have left their footprints and thrown their granite boulders across the countryside.

The Land of Lyonesse between the Scilly Isles

and Land's End is still very much there although submerged by the sea, and the bells from 140 underwater church towers sometimes ring out to be heard by those who listen well.

Piskies abound on the sea shore and on the moors and still play practical jokes on people, dangerous tricks too, for they can lead you into a bog on Bodmin Moor or make even a most accomplished sailor lose his sense of direction.

Perhaps the most enduring and outstanding facet of Cornwall is it timelessness. Tourists may come and go in their hordes. People from 'up-country' may make their holiday homes here. Modern buildings may have sprung up on the edge of many old towns and villages, pylons may march across farmland like giant robots. But despite this Cornwall's essence does not change. On the high cliffs of the North Coast or the gentler beaches of the south, on the wild and remote moorland, in the deep cut valleys, along the wide tidal river beds, it is still possible to feel as if time has only changed the surface. The days of the Celtic Saints, and the smuggling and the dreadful shipwrecks; the era of the great pilchard fishing fleets and the abundant market gardening, the mining and the Civil War battles are never faraway.

In the early part of this century picture postcards became wildly popular and hundreds of people had their albums in which to place their collections. It was in 1902 that the back of the postcard was divided for the message and the address and this saw the heyday of the cult. The hobby waned after the First World War but there was the beginning of a revival in the 1960s and in 1976 the first British International Postcard exhibition was held. Now it is the third largest collecting hobby in Britain following on after Stamps and Coins and has as many as 20,000 followers including many famous people. This book of picture postcards, mostly Edwardian taken in the early 1900s will conjure up for many how Cornish villages and towns looked in those days. The wonder remains that the atmosphere has not been blotted out by man-made alterations.

The Celtic Saints have left their Holy touch in hidden places, the toughness and the close camaraderie of miners have left their mark, the brave and intrepid seamen's souls haunt the coastline and the strong individuality of the Cornish people has stood firm and lost none of its strength.

'ONE AND ALL'

Verse 1:

Oh rugged and bold are Cornwall's cliffs,
And rugged and bold are her men,
Stalwart and true when there's work to do,
And heeding not where or when.
Braving the storm on ocean wave,
Or toiling beneath the ground.
Where-ever the spot, whatever his lot,
The Cornishman staunch is found.

Chorus:

One and all at duty's call
Shoulder to shoulder we stand or fall
On land or sea, where'er we be
We CORNISH are ready aye, ONE AND ALL.

Verse 2:

Old Cornwall is rich in her native wealth
Of copper, fish and tin,
And richer still in the strength and will,
Of the hearts that beat within.
And if ever the proud invaders' guns
Should threaten her rock-bound shore,
For Country and King her sons will be seen
ONE AND ALL in the battles' fore!

Scilly Flower Trade.
Bunching at Tresco.

The industry of flower growing must be one of the most picturesque in the world. It still goes on though hardly in the great abundance of the earlier part of the century.

It all began in the Scilly Isles where the temperate climate meant that bulbs were flowering earlier than anywhere else in the country. In 1871, it is said, a certain Mr Trevillick sent the first consignment of flowers to Covent Garden in an old hat box,

and from these humble beginnings the enterprise grew and spread to Cornwall. The 'uncrowned king' of the Scilly Isles, Augustus Smith, and his heir and nephew, Lieutenant Dorrien Smith, were instrumental in encouraging the flower farming and making it the great success it became. From January onwards everyone in the Scilly Isles was employed in the picking and bunching of flowers, and even the schools were closed during some

In the Arum Fields.
photo: T.J. King, Scilly.
151.

periods so that the children could help with the work.

The Scilly Isles lie some 28 miles west of Land's End and are by legend summits of the Lost Lands of Lyonesse, all that remains of a far larger land mass. Swinburne described the islands as a 'small sweet world of wave-encompassed wonder'. The islands have been kept totally unspoilt by the Duchy of Cornwall who have owned them since the sixteenth century. The rich and varied flora and fauna attract discerning tourists and it is now possible to reach the islands via helicopter from Penzance as well as by sea in RMMV Scillonian, a voyage that takes 2½ to 3 hours.

Over the years the Scillies have proved very dangerous, causing literally thousands of ships to be wrecked on some of the 150 or so islands, islets and rocks that make up the archipelago.

'Here on a narrow neck of land
Twixt two unbounded seas I stand.'

Wesley was reportedly standing at the cliff's edge on the ultimate point of Cornwall, Land's End, when he wrote his famous hymn. Hundreds of tourists every year visit this end of the earth. The land is being worn away by the marching feet of inquisitive people and care has had to be taken not to let the erosion go too far.

But the lure of looking out to sea from high and exciting cliffs towards the Scilly Isles will always beckon the romantics. This, to many people, is what Cornwall stands for: seas, cliffs, and the very edge of Britain. So it is from here that we set out on our journey in picture postcards. We will take you into small villages and towns working our way in zigzag fashion across and up the county of Cornwall until we meet the boundary at the River Tamar.

Through this unique collection of picture postcards we hope to show the variety of the Cornish countryside and towns. It is a nostalgic journey showing the Cornwall of eighty years ago or more. The changes in those years have probably been greater than in any other similar length of time in history. Forms of transport, modes of dress and many of Cornwall's industries, such as fishing and mining, have altered almost out of recognition. Buildings have sprung up and changed the whole shape of the land in places, in other cases familiar buildings have been brought down altering the whole look of streets and towns.

6795. 'First & Last' House, Land's End.

E 34551

Market Square, St. Just.

St Just in Penwith is the most westerly town in Cornwall and receives many of the tourists who venture here when visiting Land's End. Along the nearby cliffs may be seen the disused engine houses and the stacks of the old tin mines.

At Plan-an-Guare is the stone and earth amphi-theatre where the Cornish miracle plays were enacted and later the wrestling matches took place. With its fifteenth-century church and the dominant Methodist chapel built in 1833 and the slate hung and granite houses, St Just remains a typically Cornish town in the heart of tin mining country.

It was the painters of the Newlyn School that
made this fishermen's town world famous.
Stanhope Forbes and his friends came and settled
in Newlyn in Edwardian times and painted its
picturesque harbour and fishing boats, and the
exhibitions of their work made the town familiar
to people all over the world.

In November 1980 the Queen, Prince Philip
and Prince Andrew visited the town and admired
the still thriving fishing industry there and the
new pier.

The fishing industry is one of the oldest in Cornwall. The fishermen were famous for their independent spirit. Many of them owned their own boats which were passed from father to son. The women worked hard too helping with the unloading of the boats and with the salting and pressing of the pilchards which was the main way of preserving the fish. Since this work had to be done as soon as the fish were landed men, women and children would often work through the night.

The fisherwomen would also help to sell the fish carrying the large fishbaskets on their backs with a harness over their heads to take the weight. Round their shoulders they wore the home-woven shawls and when their men were away at sea they busied themselves knitting the famous fishermen's jerseys, often knitting at the water's edge as they waited and watched for their men to return.

*Market Jew Street, Penzance, with
the upper postcard showing the
Davy monument.*

Penzance is a town with a romance and elegance of its own. Originally a port and market town it retains these dual purposes but in Victorian times it also became well known as a holiday resort and has some fine and unusual architecture.

Market Jew Street, so named from Market Jeu (Jeudi) Thursday Market, has a monument of Humphry Davy who invented the famous miner's light. He started his career as a doctor's assistant in Penzance.

Green Market, Penzance.

Upper: The inscription on this postcard reads, 'Peace rejoicings. The end of the War. Penzance 1918'. The picture of the port side jubilations speaks for itself.
Below: Whales on the shore near Penzance. Seemingly one of the occurrences of whale suicides which drew curious but helpless on-lookers.

Upper: A portion of the British Armada of 195 warships assembled in Mount's Bay, July 1910. At this time it was the custom for ships of the British Navy to make courtesy calls on seaside ports around Britain.
Lower: One of the first motor buses arriving at Marazion Station being met by an older form of transport, the horse and cart.

Picture postcards were not only factual
pictorial accounts of the places they
depicted. They were often of an artistic
nature, recording the atmosphere of
places as much as the look.
These two cards seem to conjure up all
the hardness of life for the youngsters of
the day and the dreams they held for
better times. Taken at St Ives, one of
Cornwall's most famous fishing ports,
they show to great advantage the winding
labyrinth of narrow streets where the
fisherfolk lived before the artists and the
tourists invaded them.

Cornwall is to hundreds of people the land of beaches. Although the beaches themselves have not changed enormously, the people who come to them, their behaviour and dress have changed dramatically.

In Edwardian days everyone, both men, women and children, always seemed to wear hats, and beach huts were erected and drawn near to the water's edge by donkeys so that those brave enough to venture into the water could change discreetly out of their long and cumbersome clothes into their swimming wear. Modesty was very much the order of the day and bikini clad figures of Cornwall's beaches today would no doubt have severely shocked the Edwardian visitors.

Above: Porthminster Beach; Below: Porthmeor, both at St Ives.

Porthmeor, St. Ives

THE KNILL CELEBRATION, ST. IVES.

John Knill was a Cornishman born in 1733 at Callington. He became a bencher of Gray's Inn, secretary to Lord Buckingham, a Commissioner for the inspection of ports in the West Indies and Lord Lieutenant of Ireland. He was also made collector of customs at St Ives and, although highly suspected of rather devious practices, he was elected Mayor of that town.

He insured that the memory of his life would linger on when he built his 'folly' in the shape of a pyramid just outside the town of St Ives. Originally he hoped to be buried there but when he failed to get the ground consecrated he decided on another plan. Leaving a perpetual annuity to the mayor and burgesses of St Ives, he instructed them that each five years there should be celebrations held in his memory. Ten girls from St Ives wearing white dresses and white ribbons in their hair should sing and dance around the memorial to the music of a fiddler. The celebrations should also include a dinner given for the Mayor, the vicar, the collector of customs and their chosen friends to number nine in all.

His wishes were observed and to this day the celebrations take place to the pleasure of the local inhabitants and visitors alike.

Hayle Regatta. Sept 1909. FIRST IN. No 2 B

The small riverside towns of Cornwall have always made a great celebration out of their annual Regatta and Carnival, waterside events of this sort being particularly picturesque, and affording fun and games for the entire community.

The brass bands turned out, the women dressed up and their men put their varying boats through their paces.

The estuary of the River Hayle lies between the town and the Atlantic Ocean. In the late eighteenth century the harbour and canal were built and it became a port of some importance. Copper smelting was the mainstay of the town.

HAYLE CARNIVAL 1913. 2.

Helston Furry dance is a very ancient custom which is still celebrated every year on 8th May, and some of its customs appear to be pre-Christian. The celebrations have made the town famous throughout the land.

The morning of the Furry Dance begins with the Hal-an-Tow ceremony when a party of men and women go out into the fields to collect garlands and boughs of beech and sycamore. They return to the town singing a song which includes the lines —

'For we were up as soon as any day-O
And for to fetch the summer home,
The summer and the May-O
The summer is a come-O
The winter is a gone-O.'

As Helston Town Band plays, the dancers wend their way in and out of the houses, entering at the front door and leaving by the back. The dignitaries of the town and those who come by invitation appear in top hat and tails and the women, who are their partners, in long dresses and picture hats. The mode of dress has changed over the years as can be seen from the picture postcards. The dances start early in the morning and continue until the evening. The whole proceedings seem to generate as much enthusiasm from the local inhabitants as they ever did in ancient times when every single member of the town took part in the occasion however young, old, poor, rich or infirm.

Helston Furry Dance

Perhaps the most thrilling of the Furry Dance celebrations in this century was when the late Sir William Treloar, a Helston man who became Lord Mayor of London, came to Helston bringing the Lord Mayor's coach. In the postcard (above) he is pictured at the Helston Horse Show in May 1907. Sir Arthur Quiller Couch, that famous Cornishman of letters wrote a humorous Latin poem in honour of the Mayor's home-coming visit. Below: Meneage Street, Helston.

Two hotels that seem to conjure up the spirit of Edwardian Cornwall still exist.

The Mullion Cove Hotel (above) with its fine view over Mount's Bay and the little harbour of Mullion was once the gathering place for many show business people and famous sporting personalities. It ranked among the smartest and best loved of Cornish hotels.

Hill's Hotel (below) was owned by the Hill family of the Lizard but was eventually sold to a local brewery firm in 1951. Since then it has been run by the Greenslade family and is now known as the Lizard Hotel.

Helford Passage (above) and Gweek village
(below) offer some of the most beautiful surrounding countryside lying on the famous estuary
of the Helford River. This estuary has been made
world famous by Daphne du Maurier in her book
Frenchman's Creek which is part of this picturesque wooded river valley. The Ferry Boat Inn at
Helford Passage is still there but there has been
some new building on the waterside.

Constantine (above) and Mawnan Smith (below)
also lie above the Helford estuary. Constantine is
a hill-top village with a church not surprisingly
made from granite. Much of this hardy stone was
mined in this area.

Mawnan Smith is so named as once there were
three smithy shops in the village. The Red Lion
Inn still stands at the centre of the village
retaining its distinctive thatched roof.

Coverack lies on the wild east
coast of the Lizard Peninsula.
This was once a favourite port
with smugglers, presumably
because of the many hidden
coves and caves along the
cliffs.

St Keverne lies north of
Coverack. The picture shows the
high church spire which once
stood as a landmark to sailors
trying to avoid the treacherous
rocks of the Manacles that lie off
this coast. Buried in the churchyard are more than 400 sailors
who failed to do so.

A humorous postcard, entitled
A Cornish Beauty.
Hard to tell whether the model was male or female!

Public Buildings, Camborne

Once Camborne and Redruth were the tin mining capitals of Cornwall and although recently there have been attempts to revive tin mining it is on a far smaller scale and the industry has become a shadow of its former self. The School of Mines at Camborne has made the town world famous, and it was here that the first beam engines were used in the mines.

Dolcoath is one of the most famous and deepest mines in Cornwall. This was worked as early as 1758, before steam engines, when the extreme depth was 88 fathoms. By 1905, soon after this postcard appeared, men were mining up to 500 fathoms below the surface. The output of metallic tin increased from 2,800 tons in the early years to 14,700 tons in its heyday. It was thanks to people like Richard Trevithick, who was born at Camborne in 1771 and who invented the first high pressure steam engine, that such inventions came to be used in the mines. In 1801 Trevithick put a wheeled version of the steam engine on the road at Camborne and only a few years later was showing

it off to an admiring crowd on a track at Euston. His statue stands opposite the Public Library.

R.A.J. Walling describes a visit down Dolcoath Mine in his book **The West Country** published in 1935: 'The blackest night above the surface never gave me so intense an impression of darkness as one big stope in Dolcoath . . . It might have been a subterranean cathedral, with the whirr of the drill in the distance serving for the pedal notes of the organ, and the sound of the singing by a quartet of miners far off drifting through like a weird chant.'

He also described watching the miners descending into the mine as he stood at the head of the shaft. 'They lit their candles, stuck them in lumps of clay upon their hats, swung on to the great beam that lowered them into the mine twelve foot at a time. As they went down one struck up the melody of a hymn, and the next three to him joined in with the harmony, singing in perfect time and tune. The diminuenda as they disappeared into the darkness was something of which I had never heard the like.'

WEST END & FORE ST. REDRUTH.

Redruth once shared with Camborne the importance of being a centre of the tin and copper mining industry. Its most famous resident was William Murdoch, who married a Redruth girl and made the first gas engine here. He was the first man to experiment with gas lighting in his home in 1792. It was thanks to him that Redruth streets were lit by gas at a comparatively early stage.

THE ENTRANCE TO ILLOGAN WOODS N⁴ REDRUTH

Upper: Pool Road, Redruth in the snow with a tram
ascending the hill. Lower: The entrance to Illogan
Woods, near Redruth. The inscription on the back
of the card reads: 'Never have I seen any wood as
beautiful. It dips up and down all the way and the
pines and firs scent the air.'

Left: The docks at Portreath were built by Lord de Dunstanville, head of the Basset family who built the monument at Carn Brea in 1836. He was interested in mining and engineering and was anxious to make Portreath a port. The port was used for importing coal to Camborne and Redruth and exporting tin ore from the local mines.

Above: Porthtowan, near Redruth, a beach that remains as popular today as it obviously was in the early years of this century. Left: Portreath Hotel with passengers arriving on the country bus. The village has been greatly 'developed' and would be hardly recognisable to those who viewed it in Edwardian days. However the hotel still stands in its fine situation overlooking the unique harbour and although it no longer offers a lodging for humans or horses it is still the local pub and the centre of a very close-knit community.

Gwennap Pit, an amphitheatre carved out of a hollow formed by land subsidence from mining, has almost perfect acoustics. John Wesley made use of them and preached from here on several occasions to vast crowds of fishermen and miners. The last time he preached here was in his eighty fifth year and he had an audience of twenty thousand people.

Now it is the meeting place for the famous gathering of Methodists every Whit Monday. The lower postcard shows the Pit packed with people for one such Whit Monday service.

BILLY BRAY

"THE KING'S SON".

A NOTABLE
CORNISH MINER
AND PREACHER,

Born & Died
at
Twelve Heads
In the Parish of Kea
Near Truro.

Aged 73 Years

BALDHU CHURCH

MONUMENT ERECTED AT BALDHU
OVER THE GRAVE OF BILLY BRAY.

Billy Bray 1794-1868 was the legendary Methodist preacher of Cornwall who followed in the footsteps of John Wesley by inspiring the working people with his great oratory. He was a hard working miner himself who would often walk miles to preach in remote barns and halls. By working very long hours, sometimes 20 hours out of 24, he managed to build three chapels all in the mining area of Gwennap. He wrote, 'I would then work about the chapel by day and go to the mine at night, and had not the dear Lord greatly strengthened me for the work, I could not have done it . . . Some Sundays I had to walk twenty miles and speak three times.'

Billy Bray is remembered not only for his oratory and his zeal but for the great happiness which he derived from his faith. He spread the word of joy and salvation rather than retribution or fire and brimstone. He once wrote, 'I can't help praising the Lord. As I go along the road I lift up one foot and it seems to say "Glory", and I lift up the other and it seems to say "Amen". I can no more help praising God than the birds can help singing.'

Church Street, Falmouth

In spite of many new buildings Falmouth remains one of Cornwall's most beautifully situated towns. Its sheltered port has long given refuge to vessels caught in stormy seas. Through the narrow streets leading down to the harbour glimpses of water can be seen and it is not surprising that Sir Walter Raleigh, arriving here when there was only one dwelling and the mansion belonging to the Killigrew family, persuaded them to develop the town. The first houses must have been those in Church Street which are older than they look.

Anne Treneer wrote of Falmouth in her book **School House in the Wind**, 'In my arrogance I had thought of Falmouth (God forgive me) as a place for "visitors" and to be avoided. But when towards sunset I stood on the rocks below the lighthouse, facing the harbour, I knew that everything that had ever been written or said about the beauty of Falmouth harbour was true.'

Dockyard, fishing port and holiday resort, it meets all these descriptions and although Falmouth has recently lost much of its boat-building business it is fighting hard for the survival of these time-honoured trades.

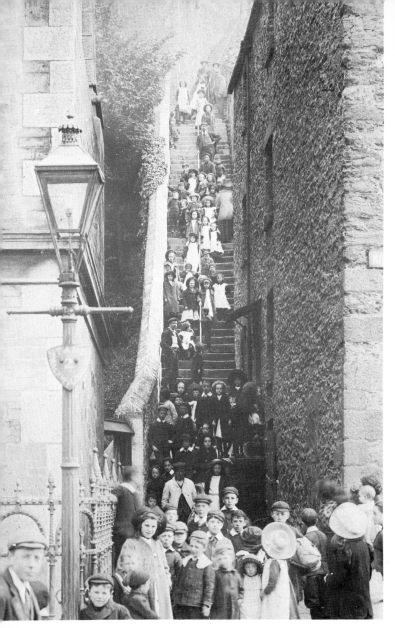

Jacob's Ladder, Falmouth

Market Street, Falmouth

Market Street, Falmouth.

Upper: Submarines in the harbour at Falmouth in 1910 before the First War. During both wars Falmouth was used a great deal by Naval ships where they not only took shelter but came for repairs. Lower: The opening of the Gyllyngdune Gardens on 5 July 1907 by the Mayor of Falmouth, Alderman J. Grose J.P. In 1896 a great deal of restoration was done on the gardens and all the Edwardian love of gardening was lavished here where many rare tropical plants were grown. Four years after the opening of the gardens, in 1911, Princess Alexander of Tech came to Falmouth to open the pavilion adjoining the gardens.

Above: Bank House which was once a home for sailors was one of the properties in Falmouth which belonged to the Fox family, the famous Quakers. It is now divided into flats. Below: **Implacable,** an eighteenth-century two deck frigate. Originally called **Duquay Trouin,** she was engaged in a battle at Trafalgar against the **Victory.** She surrendered and was brought to Plymouth to be refitted. She served for many years under the white ensign of the Mediterranean Fleet. This ship then became part of the Lion Training Establishment at Devonport but in 1908 was condemned to be sold for breaking up. An appeal was made to King Edward who granted the reprieve and thus **Implacable** arrived at Falmouth in 1910. She was refitted as a boys' holiday ship for training purposes and was eventually scuttled off Portsmouth in 1949.

Above: Gyllyngvase Beach, Falmouth as it was in 1915. Note the somewhat over-dressed holiday-makers. Donkey rides seem more of an attraction than swimming or sunbathing. Below: Penryn is an older town than its neighbour Falmouth to which it eventually lost most of its business. The houses are mainly built of granite that was mined in great quantities hereabouts and there are some outstanding examples of Georgian architecture. The King's Arms is still there and has changed hardly at all.

Mylor Village Cornwall

Mylor village is one of the most
beautifully situated in Cornwall. It stands
above Carrick Roads, the meeting of
seven rivers, and its own little Mylor
Creek. At the head of the creek is Mylor
Bridge, a popular resting place for
yachtsmen.

Ponsanooth

Ponsanooth village lies inland between
the shores of Falmouth and the wild hills
of Gwennap. In the first half of this
century there was an explosives factory
here to serve the quarries and mines
nearby.

Left: Feock is the venue for many new bungalows and other buildings. This photograph was taken by the strangely detached tower of the church. It is far more ancient than the church itself.

Below: King Harry Passage, where the ferry crosses the River Fal. It is named after King Henry VI and the passage is marked by a chapel dedicated to 'Our Lady and King Henry VI'. Some people believe it to be named after Henry VIII who reputedly stayed nearby with Anne Boleyn.

Once, as in the picture postcard, it carried horses and carts, now it carries cars. Above this reach of the river lies the grand house of Trelissick, with its beautiful gardens which are opened by the National Trust to the public.

R. Fal, The Ferry, King Harry Passage.

St. Mawes.

St. Mawes.

46

Left: St Mawes, the main town of the Roseland Peninsula, is typical of the beautifully situated towns and villages of this part of Cornwall. It is guarded from sea invasion by its own castle, a twin to Pendennis on the Falmouth side of the harbour. Both castles were built by King Henry VIII.

Small and crooked cottages, as shown in the lower postcard (left), can still be found around St Mawes and conjure up a picture of the town in its very early days.

Above: The little hamlet of Percuil once had its sense of importance. Here the horse and trap would meet those arriving by boat to take them further inland to Gerrans or Portscatho as the picture postcard shows. Probably the greatest change that has taken place since the pictures for these cards were taken is in the forms of transport which have so completely transformed the pace and style of the rest of our lives. Today when we think nothing of driving up to London it is strange to remember that it probably took as long to go from Falmouth to Gerrans by various forms of transport in Edwardian days.

47

Portscatho (above and left) has seen much new building both in Victorian times and later in the 1930s. Once, like so many other small Cornish ports, it existed solely on the fishing industry and the farming of the surrounding countryside. It was in the later Edwardian days that pilchard fishing began to die out altogether.

a Cornish Dinner Likky stew, Saffern Caake
an' a dish a tay wreth et.

Traditional foods that were enjoyed in the early
part of this century. Among the foods displayed
in these pictures only the pilchards are no longer
enjoyed in Cornwall, because these fish are not now
found in Cornish waters.

WILL EE AVE A PILCHER AN A CUP O' TAY?

Above: Truro, the only city of Cornwall and the setting for the first cathedral to be built since St Paul's in London. This picture postcard with the post date of 1904 shows the cathedral while being built. The architect was J.L. Pearson and the building took place between 1880 and 1904. J.L. Pearson died during the construction of the cathedral which was finished by his son following his father's plans. Below: St Mary's Church, which is the site of the present cathedral and part of which was incorporated into the cathedral building.

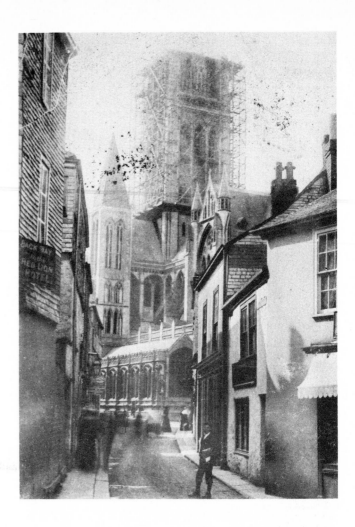

Two views of Truro's Boscawen Street. The lower
picture shows the War Memorial. The street is
named after the family of Lord Falmouth.

The viaduct at Truro which carries the railway over the valley and was replaced with granite arches in 1905.

Truro, Railway Viaduct.

Below: Another of Truro's most famous streets, upper Lemon Street. The first Lemon to make his name in the area was William Lemon who came from humble beginnings and had little education but was fascinated by mining. He brought all sorts of new ideas and machinery into the business and then spent some time educating himself. He became one of the most influential and richest men in Truro. In 1742 he was Sheriff of the County. His grandson, William Lemon junior, was knighted in 1774 and represented the county of Cornwall in Parliament during fifty years. The first William Lemon bought the house of Carclew.

The Red Lion Hotel. Once as famous as Truro's cathedral and as popular with visitors and locals alike. In 1967, after a lorry carrying a load of cement crashed into the frontage causing irreparable damage, it was demolished and is now a supermarket.

Annual bazaars and sales of work and annual outings organised by church or chapel were greatly looked forward to and enjoyed by Cornish families in the early part of this century. The custom lingers on though hardly with the same enthusiasm.

The upper postcard shows the amazing display of needlework at the Redruth Adult School Bazaar.

The lower card shows the annual Redruth Wesley Tea Treat held at Tregullow on 21 July 1904.

Upper: The St Dennis Rechabite Tea Treat in 1919. An excuse for men, women and children to don their most glamorous clothes.
Lower: The Redruth Highway Primary School Treat of July 1905. Obviously not a celebration solely for children.

Perranporth built on the north coast overlooking one of Cornwall's popular beaches. Nearby are the remains of St Piran's Church reputedly the earliest Christian building in England with walls that remain standing.

Perranporth.

Nr. Truro. Perranporth.

Above: The Wesleyan Chapel of Newlyn East abundantly decked out for Harvest Festival.
Below: The rather sombre face of the slate fronted Temperance Hotel of Newlyn East. There were many such inns in the hamlets, villages and towns at the early part of this century.

It was in Edwardian days that Newquay really
came into its own as a holiday resort. The
Atlantic Hotel and the Headland Hotel stand high
above the beach. The little bathing huts shown in
the lower picture were hauled from place to place
by donkey.

Launch of the Newquay Life Boat.

In spite of the growing importance of tourists in
Newquay the old crafts and pastimes remained.
Fishing was still one of the staple occupations and as
we see in the upper card the fish cellars still existed
where the nets and pots were kept in good condition.
Newquay's lifeboat was of paramount importance and
here we see the boat being launched in about 1913.
The annual August celebration of the launching of the
lifeboat was always a great local occasion.

59

Two views of the Beach Road, Newquay showing
the Unity fish cellar. This road was formerly
called Primrose Hill. The upper picture shows the
elegance and sophistication visitors were to lend
to Newquay. The lower picture shows the hard-
worked fisherwomen who were such a help to
their menfolk.

Above: As early as 1439 Indulgences were handed out to those prepared to help build the harbour at Newquay, so it was around the harbour that the town first grew. In 1874 a railway for goods was brought to Newquay and it became a major port for the shipping of china clay.

In the above picture we see the railway line which went into a tunnel and ran behind Fore Street, Bank Street and crossed East Street and so to the station. It was known as the Tramway. The photograph was taken well before the turn of the century.

The group of buildings on the left centre were called the Speculation Cellars. The Cosy Nook Theatre in Newquay used to be a tent erected at the left foreground. Apparently it rattled so much that the concert party could not always be heard!

The Old Mill and Bridge, Newquay.

The old Mill and Trevemper Bridge near Newquay.

Fore Street, St. Columb

Argall's Series

Bank Square, St. Columb

Argall's Series

Slate-hung houses at St Columb, home of the Hurling matches, when two teams of the toughest men of town and country battle with each other to get a silver ball through the streets to their goals outside the town. The rules date from 1750 and it is a wild and arduous competition that takes place each Shrove Tuesday.

Parish Clerk of St Columb Minor. The intricate
detail shown of the Cornish range and the chairs
and utensils of the household are most intriguing.
The picture dates from about 1908.

The Cornish pasty. Still the most loved food of the Cornish people though much maligned by many mass-produced types that are factory-baked and sold 'up country'. To sweeten the evil spirits of the mines, miners would always leave a corner of their pasty for the 'knockers' as they were called. There is also a legend that the devil would not cross the River Tamar to visit Cornwall as he was too afraid he would be cooked in a pasty. A pasty was the most convenient and nourishing food for workers to take with them and many employees would make provision for the warming of pasties at midday.

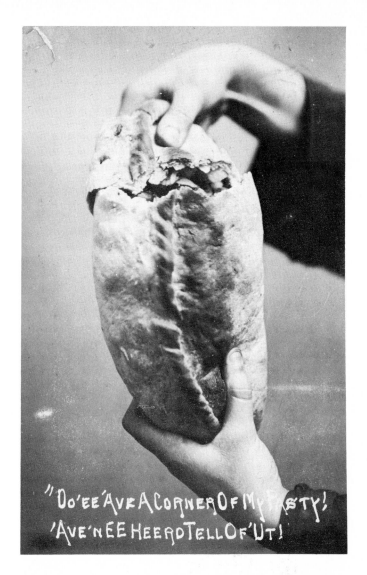

"Do'ee 'Ave A Corner Of My Pasty! 'Ave'n Ee Heerd Tell Of 'Ut!

A Cornish Compliment, Do'ee Help Yourself, There's More 'Ere Than I Can Ate

In spite of many new buildings Mevagissey retains
its magic and the atmosphere of a fishing centre.
Tucked into a steep cove on the south coast it has a
particular charm and character of its own.

The picture above shows Fore Street, Mevagissey
which was so obviously not built with the age of the
motor-car in mind.

Below, the popular annual Regatta, an event
that took place in many of the fishing villages along
the coast.

"SWIMMING MATCHES, PORTHPEAN"

PORTHPEAN

Porthpean, like Mevagissey, retains its Cornish identity. In Edwardian days the Swimming Matches were the popular local event. The picture dates from 1908 and shows the crowds this occasion attracted.

The quiet life of the villages in those days is portrayed in the lower picture.

The church tower, St. Austell

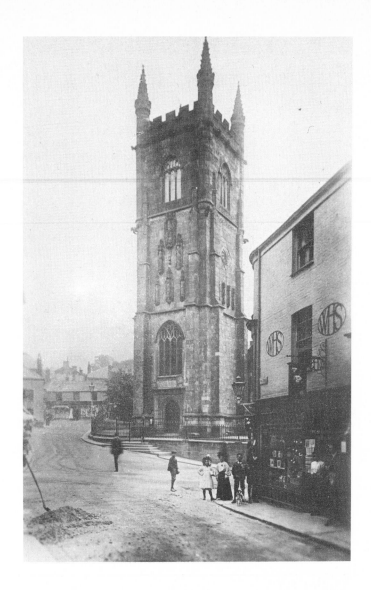

Wesleyan Church and Victoria Road
Mount Charles, St Austell

Fore Street, St Austell

St Austell was originally a town centred on the surrounding tin mining until the extraction of china clay took over as the main industry of the area in the early nineteenth century. The church of St Austell is one of the most beautiful in Cornwall with its elaborately carved fifteenth-century tower standing proudly above the town.

Holiday visitors venture here from the surrounding resorts and the town offers some fine shopping facilities. The china clay industry has made it a prosperous and self-sufficient town.

Two famous men were instrumental in the finding and furthering of the china clay industry. William Cookworthy of Plymouth, a chemist and potter who as early as 1746 identified the substance as china clay or kaolin, and later Josiah Wedgewood.

Great hills and peaks of white slag, the waste from china clay extraction, litter the countryside around St Austell and have a weird beauty and attraction of their own that make up part of Cornwall's historical backdrop. Daphne du Maurier described them as 'living monuments to the audacity and courage of generations of working men'.

St Dennis, another town greatly affected by the china clay industry, since the surrounding area is most prolific in china clay.

Luxulyan Village

70

The Dock Gates, Charlestown.

Luxulyan Village, (below, left) is situated in one of Cornwall's most beautiful valleys surrounded by granite bouldered moors and with thick vegetation towards the narrowing of the valley. Here stands the great Treffry viaduct built in 1839 of granite from the surrounding countryside as are the houses of the village, and the unusually large church. Porphyry is the type of granite particular to this valley which was used for the monument of the Duke of Wellington in St Paul's Cathedral and also for a hall in Place House, Fowey, home of the Treffry family.

Charlestown (above) became famous when Charles Rashleigh built the harbour here in 1791. The port was renamed in his honour, as previously it had been called West Polmear. It has long been one of the main harbours for shipping quantities of china clay mined in the adjacent countryside. In Edwardian days many schooners came to the harbour escorted by tugs and were pulled into the inner harbour basin by lines when the inner gates were opened.

Philip Varcoe, whose family have been for generations involved with the china clay industry, wrote in his little history of china clay: 'The harbour master had a bell and whistle, as well as a splendid voice, and the shouts and noise of running chains and hawsers, creaking decks and ship sides were wonderful to hear. Charlestown has changed so little during the past 150 years.'

Fowey is one of the most picturesque towns in Cornwall. In spite of the fact that it attracts many tourists and visitors year after year, it has retained its character, and the atmosphere of the place has changed very little.

It has been for many years one of the main ports from which china clay is shipped, trains bringing their cargo of clay to the very waterside. Before that there was always an association with sea-going vessels: every kind of ship from trading vessels to privateers, from smugglers to warships, including those belonging to the French and the Spanish who came to raid the town.

Drake sailed from here to the West Indies and fishermen put to sea from the Haven of Fowey to catch their pilchards. Sir Arthur Quiller-Couch who lived here for most of his life made the town world famous for it is the 'Troy Town' of his novels.

The view from Hall Walk on the Bodinnick side of the Ferry is one of the most breathtaking to be seen in Cornwall. The photograph above was taken in 1912. Almost three hundred years earlier Carew, in his famous **Survey of Cornwall**, described the view like this: 'In passing along, your eyes shall be called away from guiding your feet, to descry by their farthest kenning the vast ocean speckled with ships that continually this way trade forth and back to most quarters of the world. Nearer home, they take view of all sized cocks, barges, and fisher-boats, hovering on the coast. Again, contracting your sight to a narrower scope, it lighteth on the fair and commodious haven, where the tide daily present-eth his double service of flowing and ebbing, to carry and recarry whatsoever the inhabitants shall be pleased to charge him withall, and his creeks (like a young wanton lover) fold about the land with many embracing arms.'

Today the description still fits exactly.

Fowey town consists of winding narrow streets leading to the harbour below and life revolves around the waterside. Many of the old houses still exist such as the Old Lugger Inn in the upper postcard. At Fowey china clay is loaded onto ships that take this valuable commodity all over the world. The lower photograph was taken in 1909 showing how busy the industry was at that time.

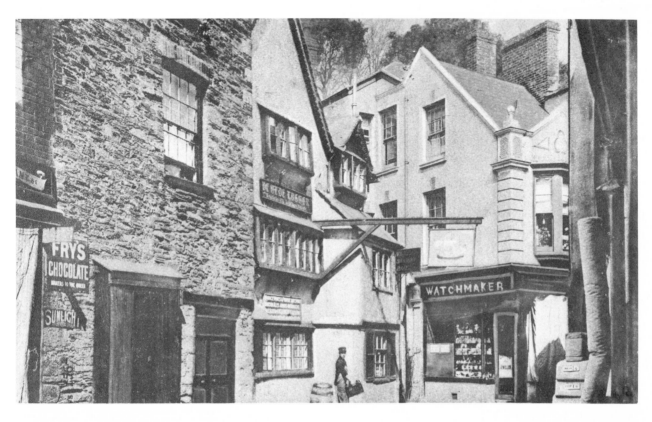

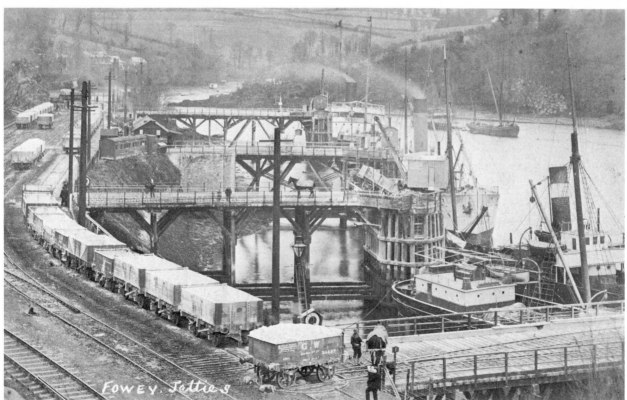

Lostwithiel Street, Fowey

BODINNICK FERRY, FOWEY

Across the water from Fowey is the little hamlet of Bodinnick. There are some new houses now built on the hill above but the little street that meets the ferry which passes constantly from Fowey to Bodinnick is still much the same as it was when these photographs were taken. At that time the ferry carried horses and carts and pedestrians, now in the summer months it is constantly full of cars.

In the upper photograph the house on the right has belonged for many years to the du Maurier family. They bought it when Daphne and her sisters, Angela and Jeanne, were young girls. Angela du Maurier still lives there and is a much loved member of the community.

75

The village of Golant lies on the banks of the
Fowey river on the last reaches of the wide
estuary. There has been a lot of building since
these photographs were taken in the early years
of this century, but many of the old houses still
exist and form the character of the place. It is the
little church of Golant, perched above the village
that is said to be where King Mark celebrated his
reconciliation with Iseult and she bequeathed her
dress to the church as a memento. This is the
church named after the great Celtic Saint
Sampson who travelled across Cornwall con-
verting heathens and killing snakes with equal
bravado.

Golant is still a home for fishermen and a
famous family of boatbuilders named Tabb and
some retired people who have chosen this peace-
ful end-of-the-road village for their final retreat.

Lerryn is a pretty village sitting either side of the river of the same name which is a tributary of the River Fowey. The woods here touch the water at high tide and when the tide is out the shining mud-flats are the playground of many species of birds. Sailing boats brought their wares as far as Lerryn in Edwardian days where they were off-loaded.

For many years before the first World War and between the wars, Lerryn Regatta (upper postcard) was one of the most colourful events of this part of Cornwall. People rowed here from their riverside homes from miles about to join in this enjoyable and highly competitive occasion.

Those who still remember them talk of the regatta days with great nostalgia. For many people living in Lerryn and other riverside villages, their boats were their only form of transport. So the cele-brations which centred around these waterside events were of enormous importance and enjoyment.

THE OLD CORNISH FISH SELLER.

POLLOCK, POLLOCK, WHITING, MACKEREL!!!

"LIKE BARS OF SILVER"

Gone are the days when the sound of the calls of fish sellers (left) were a constant background to everyday life but are still remembered with affection by a few elderly inhabitants of seaside or river estuary towns. Cornish fishermen lived an arduous life but were a proud and independent group of men.

"When the Boats come in."

CORNISH FISHERMEN

Lostwithiel is a friendly compact little town built by the River Fowey at the point where it becomes tidal. It is steeped in history being so close to Restormel Castle. There are the remains of the Duchy Palace built by Earl Edmund of Cornwall and once this was a major port and stannary town before the river silted up. Now the slim spire of St Bartholomew Church dominates the sky line. The church dates from the fourteenth century and during the Civil War Royalist prisoners were kept here by the Parliamentarians.

Because the main road runs on the outskirts of the town the centre is unspoilt and one can wander there and enjoy the many beautiful buildings without the disturbance of traffic. Lostwithiel people are proud of their heritage and run their own little museum which has much to tell about the old capital of Cornwall.

Bodmin is the official County town of Cornwall and the Assize Courts is one of the most outstanding buildings designed by a local architect from Launceston called Burt. It was built in 1837.

The town once had a terrible gaol where it was said the people of Bodmin could watch the public executions taking place from the opposite hill.

But Bodmin was originally a religious centre and the name derives from 'bod-minachan' meaning the abode of Monks. It was here that St Petroc founded a priory in the sixth century. In the church of Bodmin St Petroc's remains are kept in an ivory casket. The church is one of the largest in Cornwall with a fine Norman font and the churchyard has a special atmosphere which seems appropriate to its hundreds of years of religious connections.

Bodmin Hill, Lostwithiel

*Fore Street,
Bodmin*

Honey Street, Bodmin

81

Wadebridge, built on the wide estuary of the
River Camel, is famous for its great bridge.
Arthur H. Norway wrote: 'When the tide is out, it
is as though the town had lost its soul.'

Once there was a ford across the river which
was replaced by a stone bridge as early as the
fifteenth century, the building of which was
organised by the Vicar of Egloshayle. It has since
been widened twice.

Molesworth Street, the main street, is named
after the family of that name who lived at
Pencarrow between Wadebridge and Bodmin. It
was at this house in 1882 that Sir Arthur
Sullivan composed some of the music for
Iolanthe. The photographs date from 1905.

The picture postcards depict the Reverend William Iago and the Reverend Sabine Baring-Gould of Lewtrenchard taking part in the excavations of an Iron Age cemetery at Harlyn Bay, under the direction of Mr Reddie Mallet, between 1900 and 1905. It was one of the most exciting archaeological finds of the century disclosing over 130 individual graves, many skeletons and some rare pieces of metalwork.

Workmen (left) uncovering a group of cists which were examined by scientists (below)

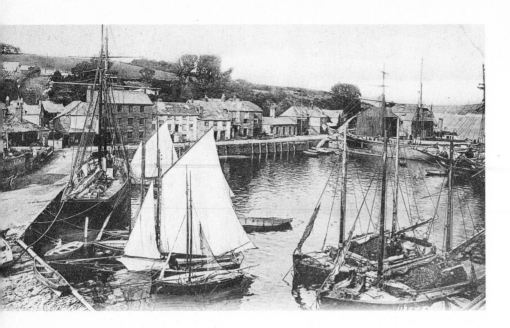

Padstow Harbour

Paddle steamer at Padstow

Market Place, Padstow

The Hobby Horse on May Day

Padstow lies further down the Camel estuary from Wadebridge towards the sea. It is an old fishing port and was for many years a shipbuilding centre. The slate-hung houses and old harbour retain their secluded atmosphere. In Edwardian times the railway was brought here from Wadebridge and it became a favourite port for holiday visitors. A ferry has run from Padstow to Rock since the fourteenth century.

Trips on paddle steamers were a great recreation much enjoyed in Victorian and Edwardian times. The beautiful lines of these paddle steamers is shown in the postcard (left).

Above is a picture dating from 1906 of the Padstow Hobby Horse carnival which takes place annually on May Day. The custom is of ancient origin dating back to pre-Christian times. More recently in the fourteenth century, when many of the Padstow men were away fighting in Calais, the town was attacked by a French ship and its men. The people of Padstow dressed up a terrifying effigy of a hobby horse, took it down to the harbour and successfully frightened the enemy away. Since then the Hobby Horse has been taken through the streets of Padstow annually, its dance promising the coming of summer and of fertility for the women of the town. Over the years the custom has been widely criticised as 'improper and carnal' but the dance continues each year accompanied by song and music played on an accordian.

Port Gaverne on the north coast has a popular
bathing beach in a sheltered cove. The criss
cross of hills behind the village make a dramatic
back drop.

Port Isaac with its winding
narrow streets is an old fishing
port once engaged with the
prolific pilchards, now turning
more to shell fish. It is often
considered the north coast's most
picturesque village.

Some say the name Camelford derives from Camelot and nearby is the Slaughterbridge where in 542, so it is said, King Arthur was mortally wounded at the battle of Camlann. From such legends the town has managed to claim a romance of its own.

Delabole, just west of Camelford, is the site of the huge quarry where the famous Cornish slate of the same name is extracted. Delabole slate has been used for many houses in the county both for roofing and as wall cladding. The great scars left by the quarrying give the place a haunted atmosphere made even stronger by a backdrop of both sea and moor.

I visited Slaughter Bridge Ian Potts' wife's family home is nearby - very old Elizabethan - low ceiling very dark. Was setting for the first Polgarth series.

The little inland village of Trelights, approached
by narrow secluded lanes and with its slate-hung
houses and Methodist Chapel, is typical of the
best of Cornwall's countryside.

Trelights Village, St. Endellion, Cornwall.
T. Harris's Series, Quethiock, Liskeard.

Bossiney village (right), just north of Tintagel,
once boasted a castle of its own and is built
around the surviving mound. Until 1832 Bossiney
returned its own member of Parliament and Sir
Francis Drake was once its representative.
Now its attraction is that it is less developed than
neighbouring Tintagel, but still abounds with
romantic legend of Celtic Saints and Arthurian
knights.

Tintagel. *Village Trevona.*

With its castle, the abounding legends of King
Arthur, and the really stupendous views along the
coastline, Tintagel (above) has become one of the
most popular places in Cornwall for tourists. It
has been totally changed since the above picture
was taken. On the left stands the Old Post Office
with its irregular walls and sloping bent roof, the
oldest building in the village and said to be part
of the fourteenth-century Manor House.

St Mabyn (above) and St Teath (below) both
boast fine fifteenth-century churches. The one at
St Mabyn may be seen from miles around as the
village is perched high on the hill top. Both
places are surrounded by unforgettable countryside leading down to the River Allen, a tributary
of the Camel.

The picture of Trebarwith dates from 1906. The
road seems to lead straight into the sea passing
'Good Stabling' and the inevitable inns. Across
the water stands Gull Rock.

Lanlivery, Ancient Celtic Cross.

Two of the grand old Cornish Crosses which are
dotted around the countryside in unlikely and
picturesque settings. Many mark the visitation of a
Celtic Saint who passed nearby, and some the
existence of later Christians who came to the
places where the hermits first lived and practised
their religion.

Quethiock Cross.

Brown Willy is the highest point on Bodmin Moor and in the county. It lies next to Roughtor — from where it is viewed in the above postcard — in the midst of the moor not far from Bolventor. The bleak and undeniable beauty of this boggy marshland may be seen from the A30 when driving from Launceston to Bodmin.

Farmers who lived in remote farmsteads on this bleak land and who managed to make a living from its barren soil were characters of great strength and fortitude. Sadly, but understandably, many have left to make their living under less arduous circumstances. There are only a few left who still dig the peat from the moorland, as these men do in the picture postcard, to burn in their open granite fireplaces, and who have learned to love this secluded and starkly beautiful land.

The moor has been deserted, not only by the gallant farmers, but by the miners who came to dig for tin and copper and the quarry men who carved out the granite.

Some find the moor too eerie to enjoy. It is dangerous ground to travel on alone when the low mists fall so suddenly, and the boggy land of new born rivers cannot be properly discerned, and the winds howl frighteningly. But to walk upon the moor on bright clear days, to see the shadows of the clouds skud across the bracken, the heather and the granite tors is to see Cornwall's heart exposed in all its glory.

Minions (above right) is truly a moorland place for, situated on the east of Bodmin Moor at more than 1,000 feet, it is the highest village in Cornwall. Once this was the home of the copper miners who worked on the nearby mines during the copper boom which was going strong in Edwardian times.

St Neot (below) lies on the south of the moor. It is a pretty place with a beautiful church containing some of the finest and earliest stained glass in the country. Around the village the Civil War raged and the custom is still maintained of hanging a bough on the church tower to commemorate the time King Charles hid in a tree nearby to escape the Parliamentarians.

Crow's Nest, St. Cleer, Nr. Liskeard.

"Cornish Village" Seri

St Cleer (above left) is another moorland village once largely inhabited by copper miners working on the famous and lucrative copper mine at Caradon Hill. It remains my favourite moorland village with its expansive views over the moor down the valley to Liskeard.

Not far from the village stands the great granite formation called the Cheesewring, with its flat weathered slabs of granite so precariously balanced upon each other. If you walk to the Cheesewring from St Cleer you will pass the 'Hurlers', circles of standing stones which date from the Bronze Age. Nearby is Trethevy Quoit the grandest chamber tomb on the moor.

This moorland expanse seems to jumble the passing of time most strangely so that Megalithic tombs and Bronze Age standing stones and St Cleer's fifteenth century church and the ruins of copper mines and engine houses are all intermingled. In a strange way they seem to make ancient history part of the present and today already as old as time.

Crow's Nest (below left) is an attractive hamlet close to St Cleer and hidden from the rest of the world along lanes with high banks. Life seems to have changed little here.

At Blisland stands a modern monument, a rock carving done in 1809 by a certain John Rogers which is called the Jubilee Rock. Blisland village itself has a large and most un-Cornish village green and a magnificent fifteenth century church.

Southgate Arch, Launceston.

98

Launceston has long been known as the Gateway to Cornwall, overlooking Polson Bridge, until recently the main crossing of the River Tamar into Cornwall.

In medieval days the town was surrounded by walls, now all that is left of them is the Southgate Arch. In the thirteenth century the rooms above the arch were used as a guard room. Hundreds of years later in the early part of the nineteenth century they were a terrible gaol, named the Dark House.

In 1887, Mr Richard Peter, one of Launceston's most respected citizens, completely restored the Southgate building in celebration of Queen Victoria's jubilee. He did a fine job and it is partly due to him that the building remains the glory of the town.

In 1960 it was feared that the tree which so strangely grew from the grey stone walls would damage the archway and so it was removed, much to the chagrin of the local residents.

But Southgate Arch remains an exciting and uniquely beautiful entrance to the narrow streets of Launceston.

Upper: Launceston Market Square, the centre of
the town, surrounded by a variety of vehicles.
Carts, carriages and cars. Transport was just beginning to change rapidly. The Butter Market was
later replaced by the war memorial. Lower: The
countryside surrounding Launceston is some of the
most secluded in Cornwall, like a piece of no-man's
land. Egloskerry Ford is typical of some of the un-
touched, out-of-the-way places in this area that still
hold a magic of their own.

Frank Trewin, Jeweller, Ironmonger and Cycle Agent, Kilkhampton, Cornwall.

One of the ways of using the popular picture post-cards at this time was as a form of advertising. Mr Trewin of Kilkhampton obviously sold a huge variety of items in his shop (above). Printed on the back of the card is the notice on the right.

The Right House at the Right Price

FOR
Watches, Clocks, Jewellery, Electro-plate, Cutlery, Guns, Cartridges.

Agent for all THE BEST BICYCLES.

Ironmongery, Enamelled Goods, Tinware, Brushes, Lamps.

ALL KINDS OF MIXED PAINTS.

Methylated & Motor Spirits, Turpentine, Alexandra & Royal Daylight Lamp Oils, Machine and Linseed Oils.

A Trial Order respectfully solicited.

The ladies' bathing beach at Bude

The Strand, Bude

Before Bude (left) became a major seaside resort its first claim to fame was as the port for the famous Bude Canal, built in 1819. There was an enormous amount of traffic along this canal which was built primarily to take sea sand as fertiliser to the inland farms in the district. In the 1890s the London and South Western Railway came to Bude and brought to an end the trade on the canal.

The town has some fine beaches and a famous golf course, and is the major resort in the area.

Poughill (below) lies to the north of Bude and in its church is an inscription to Sir Goldsworthy Gurney who built the small castle in Bude and was a famous inventor. The inscription reads: 'His inventions and discoveries in steam and electricity made communication by land and sea so rapid that it became necessary for all England to keep uniform time.'

The collier **Nivelle** of London which went aground in fog between Pentreath Bay and Lizard Point on 10 June 1923. The crew of twenty were saved by the Lizard lifeboat.

The Southampton collier **Rosedale** which went aground in November 1893 at Porthminster Beach, St Ives. There were several shipwrecks in the storms of this fateful day for seagoing vessels.

The **Gunvor**, a Norwegian 1,491 ton steel barque, wrecked at Black Head, south of Coverack, 6 April 1912. The ship was the largest sailing ship to be wrecked on Black Head. She grounded so close in that the crew were able to escape to the shore by climbing out onto the bow. There were more than a dozen wrecks on the south coast of Cornwall that year.

Liskeard, Fore Street.

Liskeard market town has some of the most
beautiful town houses in Cornwall. With the
prosperity the copper mines of Caradon brought to
the area, many distinguished Georgian and Victorian houses were built here.

Bay Tree Hill,
Liskeard

Liskeard is built on the steep sides of a valley and
the shops wend their way down in an attractive
way to the bottom of this valley, Brunel built one
of his famous stone viaducts in the valley below
and although it is now a ruin it is still a
commanding sight. Since the by-pass has been
opened the once heavy rumble of traffic through
the main street has gone and the place is more
serene though remaining a main shopping centre.

Church Street,
Liskeard

Menheniot Village.

Menheniot,

MENHENIOT POST OFFICE

Menheniot lies in the beautiful hinterland between
Liskeard and Saltash. The combination of fields,
high narrow winding lanes and wooded copses
makes this part of Cornwall one of the most
attractive and least spoilt.

If you drive from Callington along the foot of Kit Hill you dip down to the valley and Gunnislake town is perched there by the River Tamar, the great divide between Devon and Cornwall. This town was once full of tin, copper and silver miners.

When the mines collapsed in the early part of this century hundreds of them migrated all over the world seeking out more prosperous mines where they could use their skills.

Launceston Road, Callington.

The character of Callington has changed little over the years although extensive building is taking place all the time on its outskirts. It is still essentially a market town and, although many 'foreigners' from up-country have moved here, it has a caring, close-knit community. Once the granite quarries and tin mines at nearby Kit Hill brought their own trade and life to the little town. Now there is an industrial estate on its outskirts and renewed interest in reworking the mines of the area.

Upper: Coads Green, another hidden village of Cornwall. Traffic passes through on its way from Callington to Bodmin Moor and elsewhere but little else has come to change the peace of the hamlet. Nearby runs the River Lynher, one of Cornwall's most beautiful and perhaps least known rivers.

Lower: Stoke Climsland is also situated in the Lynher valley. The great character of this town in recent history was Canon Martin Andrews, who came as Vicar in 1922 and stayed there until 1968.

He started up a huge market garden industry under the auspices of the then Prince of Wales which did a great deal to alleviate the problem of local unemployment in the late 1920s and early 1930s. He filled the fifteenth-century church with his inspired preaching and his love of the community here was legendary. He retired to Downderry where he now lives and at 95 years of age is still spreading his own particular brand of joyful enthusiasm for life to the hundreds of Cornish people he has befriended over the years from every walk of life.

Calstock is built on the steep slope down to the great River Tamar just down river from Gunnislake. In Victorian and Edwardian days this was a very busy river town with all kinds of traffic constantly passing on the water. It was here on the Devon banks that James Goss had his boat-yard which can be seen in the picture postcard below. At this time the majestic viaduct was in the process of being built. When the viaduct was finished in 1906 the coming of the steam train put a stop to much of the river traffic and meant the end of James Goss's boatyard.

The ferry in the picture (right) once ran constantly from the Ferry Inn on the Devon banks to the Cornish side. In amongst the tiered houses are strips of land, part of the great market gardens here about. There were many more in Edwardian days but some still survive.

CALSTOCK VIADUCT.

Polperro

Downderry

Downderry Village.

112

Whitesand Bay (below) is one of the most popular beaches of the south coast. When the tide is out the white sands stretch for miles and though the walk down the steep cliff is wearisome, and more so on the upward return journey, it still attracts hundreds of people in the summer time.

Polperro and Downderry (left), two seaside resorts of the south coast which have been plundered by tourists who come in the summer months. To see them at their best one should go in the spring, winter or autumn. The little harbour at Polperro is breathtakingly beautiful on a deserted winter's day. It is foremost a fisher port and its steep extremely narrow streets are no place for cars. It has also attracted many artists because of its picturesque setting.

Downderry too attracts seasonal visitors and has some really fine sea views stretching down the coastline towards the Lizard.

Hessenford Mill in the wooded valley that follows
the Seaton river which winds its way towards the
sea and a holiday village. The Mill is now the Post
Office.

Polbathic, Near St. Germans.

Both Polbathic and Hessenford are neighbours of St Germans which Sir John Betjeman described as 'a kingdom of its own'. Polbathic is a hamlet of stone houses edged by a beautifully wooded tidal creek but now totally disturbed by the main road which passes through it.

Hessenford.

Forder — Near Saltash

Forder village lies on a creek of the Lynher River where it runs to meet the River Tamar. It is at the bottom of a steep hill that leads to Trematon Castle, one of the best preserved of Cornwall's Norman castles. It became a favourite with the first Duke of Cornwall, the Black Prince.

In the nearby town of Saltash is the house where Sir Francis Drake's first wife, Mary Newman, lived. It is in a street just above the famous Brunel railway bridge, and the more modern road bridge.

116

The Ferry Bridge, Saltash.

The two famous ferries that once carried all the passengers from the Devon banks to the Cornish shores between Devonport and Torpoint and Plymouth and Saltash. The Saltash ferry has been replaced by the great toll bridge opened in 1961 but the Torpoint ferry still runs. The photographs date from 1915.

TORPOINT AND FERRY. DEVONPORT.

Fore Street, Saltash

Saltash Fore Street taken in 1906. Saltash is a much older town than Plymouth and the old song goes:—

Saltash was a borough town
When Plymouth was a furzy down.

Saltash was a port for tin and a famous fishing centre and held the Liberty of the Waters Tamar. Now it is in danger of losing its character altogether as its outskirts become smothered in houses built as a dormitory for those who work in Plymouth. There are some fine Victorian houses built on the quiet side of the town looking over the Hamoaze which affords some panoramic views. The station is now hardly in use though it knew its heyday when the Brunel bridge came into existence in 1859.

Many buildings suffered in the war and others were removed to make way for the traffic crossing the new toll bridge. Strange to think that in the seventeenth century this town was described by Carew as 'consisting of three streets, which every shower washeth clean'.

Two views of Brunel's bridge at Saltash

Gore Street Hill, Saltash.

5. THE STATION, SALTASH

ALSO AVAILABLE

FOLLOWING THE TAMAR

by Sarah Foot. 63 photographs and map. Price £1.20.
Sarah Foot is the Tamar's inevitable author, living only a mile from its banks, seeing it every day from her Cornish home, and truly loving it.
'. . . both a labour of love and a work of subtle selection, combining the intriguing byways of local history and geography with a profusion of well-chosen black and white plates.'
Dick Benson-Gyles, The Western Evening Herald

MY GRANDFATHER ISAAC FOOT

by Sarah Foot. 58 photographs. Price £1.75.
A true crusader, Isaac Foot was a radical, uncompromising Liberal, a staunch Methodist and an eloquent orator and lawyer.
'. . . a rich harvest of information.'   Cornwall Courier
'. . . entirely enchanting . . .'   Alan Gibson, The Spectator
'An affectionate account . . .'   The Sunday Telegraph

LEGENDS OF CORNWALL

by Sally Jones. 60 photographs and drawings. Price £1.50.
Brilliantly illustrated with photographs and vivid drawings of legendary characters. A journey through the legendary sites of Cornwall, beginning at the Tamar and ending at Land's End.
'Highly readable and beautifully romantic . . .'
Desmond Lyons, Cornwall Courier

KING ARTHUR COUNTRY in CORNWALL, THE SEARCH for the REAL ARTHUR

by Brenda Duxbury, Michael Williams and Colin Wilson.
Over 50 photographs and 3 maps. Price £1.20.
An exciting exploration of the Arthurian sites in Cornwall and Scilly, including the related legends of Tristan and Iseult, with The Search for the Real Arthur by Colin Wilson.
'. . . provides a refreshing slant on an old story linking it with the present.'
Caroline Righton. The Packet Newspapers

MY CORNWALL

A personal vision of Cornwall by eleven writers living and working in the county: Daphne du Maurier, Ronald Duncan, James Turner, Angela du Maurier, Jack Clemo, Denys Val Baker, Colin Wilson, C.C. Vyvyan, Arthur Caddick, Michael Williams and Derek Tangye, with reproductions of paintings by Margo Maeckelberghe and photographs by Bryan Russell. Price £1.50.
'An ambitious collection of chapters.'
The Times, London

SUPERNATURAL IN CORNWALL

by Michael Williams. 24 photographs. Price £1.75.
'. . . a book of fact, not fiction . . . covers not only apparitions and things that go bump in the night, but also witchcraft, clairvoyancy, spiritual healing, even wart charming . . .'
Jenny Myerscough on BBC
'Serious students of ghost-hunting will find a fund of locations.'
Graham Danton on Westward TV

FOLLOWING THE RIVER FOWEY

by Sarah Foot. 49 photographs. Price £1.
Sarah Foot follows the Fowey from its beginnings on Bodmin Moor to where it meets the sea beyond Fowey and Polruan.
'She stitches into the simple tapestry of the river's story names and incidents and anecdotes, deftly and lovingly, every thread and every page touched with charm and an unashamed sense of delight.'
Western Morning News

OCCULT IN THE WEST

by Michael Williams. Over 30 photographs. Price £1.75.
Michael Williams follows his successful **Supernatural in Cornwall** with further interviews and investigations into the Occult — this time incorporating Devon. Ghosts and clairvoyancy, dreams and psychic painting, healing and hypnosis are only some of the facets of a fascinating story.
'. . . provides the doubters with much food for thought.'
Jean Kenzie, Tavistock Gazette

POLDARK COUNTRY

by David Clarke, over 80 photographs. Price £1.20.
Fascinating facts about the Cornish past, locations used for the TV series and interviews with Winston Graham and the cast.

MAKING POLDARK

by Robin Ellis. Over 60 photographs. Price £1.20.
The inside story of the popular BBC TV series.
'. . . an interesting insight into the making of the TV series . . .'
Camborne Redruth Packet
'It is a "proper job", as they say, and a credit to all concerned.'
Archer in Cornwall Courier

THE CRUEL CORNISH SEA

by David Mudd. 65 photographs. Price: £1.75.
David Mudd selects more than 30 Cornish shipwrecks, spanning 400 years, in his fascinating account of seas and a coastline that each year claim their toll of human lives.
'This is an important book.'
Lord St Levan, the Cornish Times

CASTLES OF CORNWALL

by Mary and Hal Price. 78 photographs and map.
Price: Hardcover £3.75. Paperback £1.75.
St Catherine's Castle and Castle Dore both at Fowey, Restormel near Lostwithiel, St Mawes, Pendennis at Falmouth, St Michael's Mount, Tintagel, Launceston and Trematon near Saltash. Mary and Hal Price on this tour of Cornwall explore these nine castles.
'. . . a lavishly illustrated narrative that is both historically sound and written in a compelling and vivid style that carries the reader along from one drama to the next.'
Pamela Leeds, The Western Evening Herald

CORNISH MYSTERIES

by Michael Williams. 40 photographs. Price £1.50.
Cornish Mysteries is a kind of jig-saw puzzle in words and pictures. The power of charming, mysterious shapes in the Cornish landscape, the baffling murder case of Mrs Hearn are just some fascinating ingredients.
'. . . superstitions, dreams, murder, Lyonesse, the legendary visit of the boy Jesus to Cornwall, and much else. Splendid, and sometimes eerie, chapters.'
The Methodist Recorder

We shall be pleased to send you our catalogue giving full details of our growing list of titles for Devon and Cornwall and forthcoming publications.

If you have difficulty in obtaining our titles, write direct to Bossiney Books, Land's End, St Teath, Bodmin, Cornwall. Books 95p and over add 50p for posting and packing, books under 95p add 30p, hardcovers add 75p.